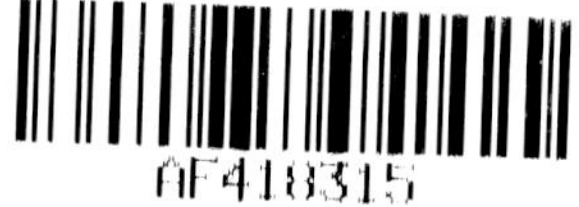

PFERDE MALBUCH

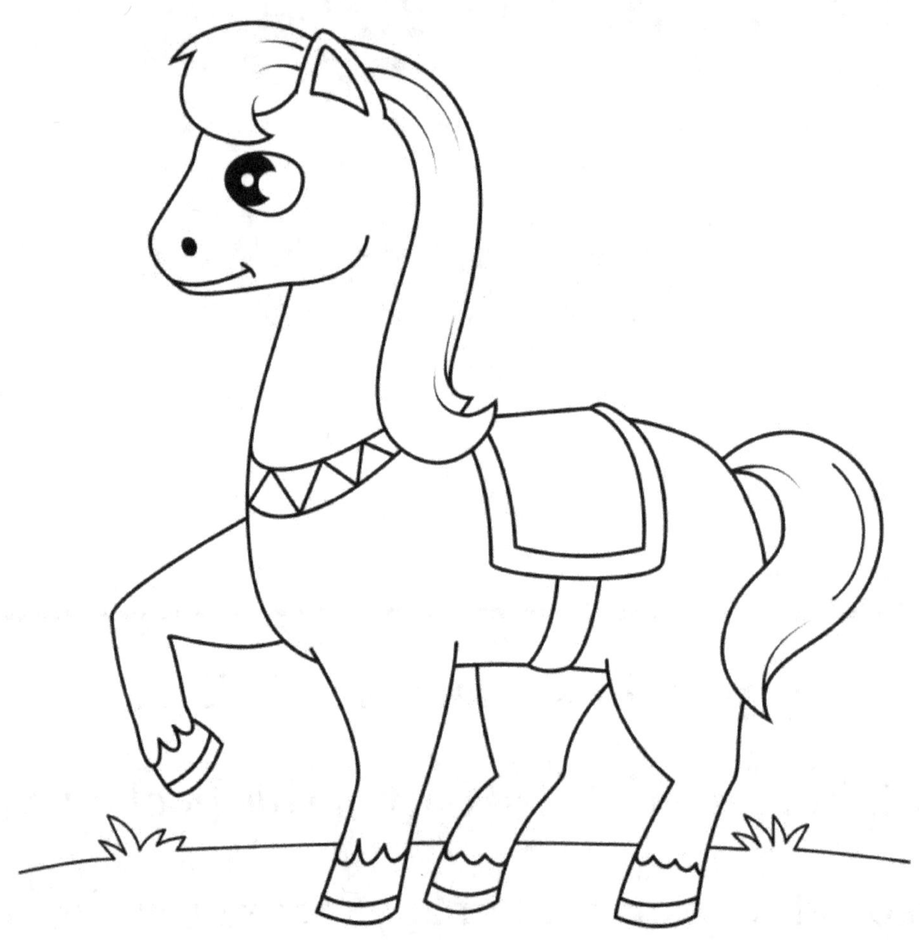

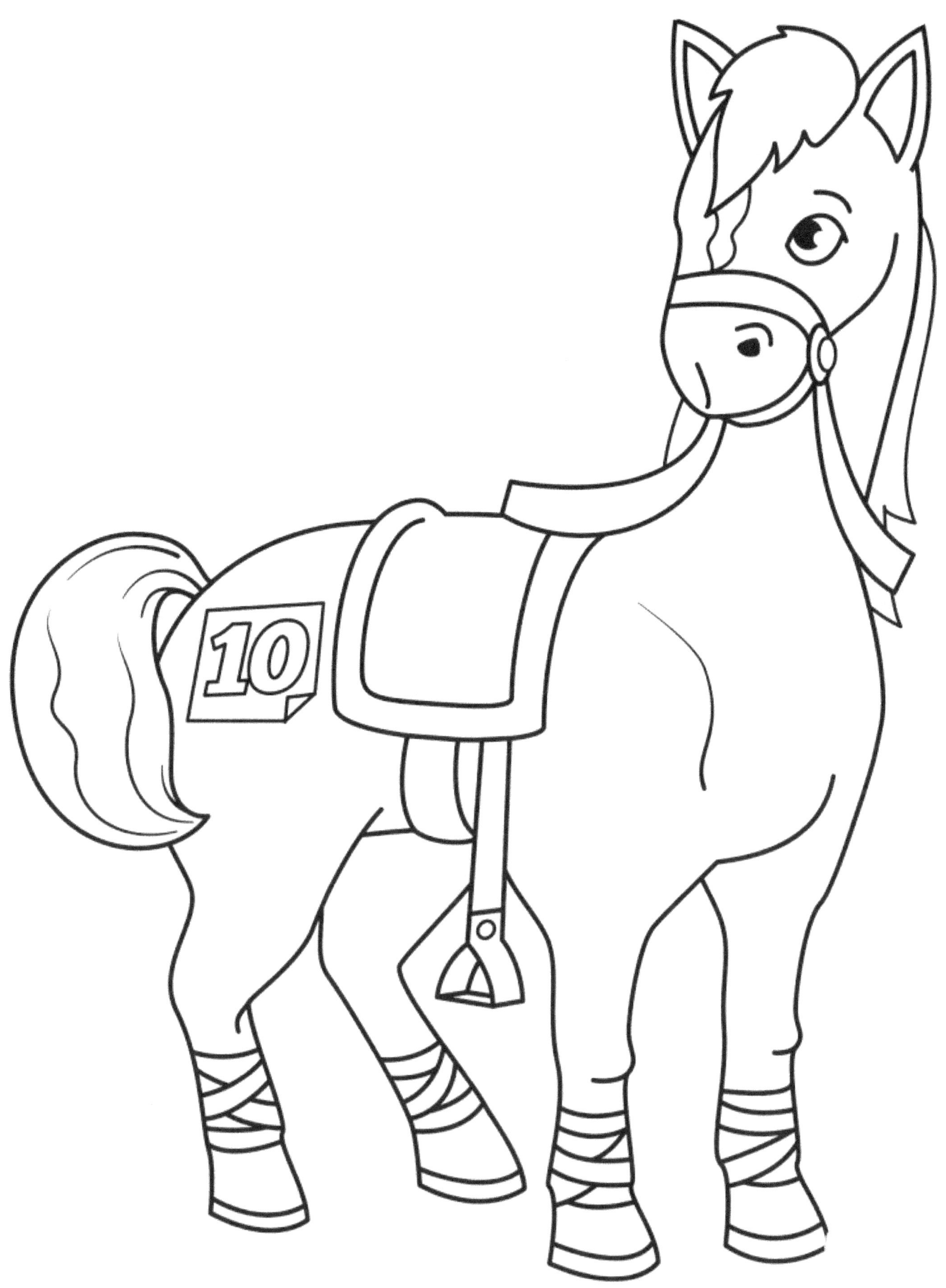

10

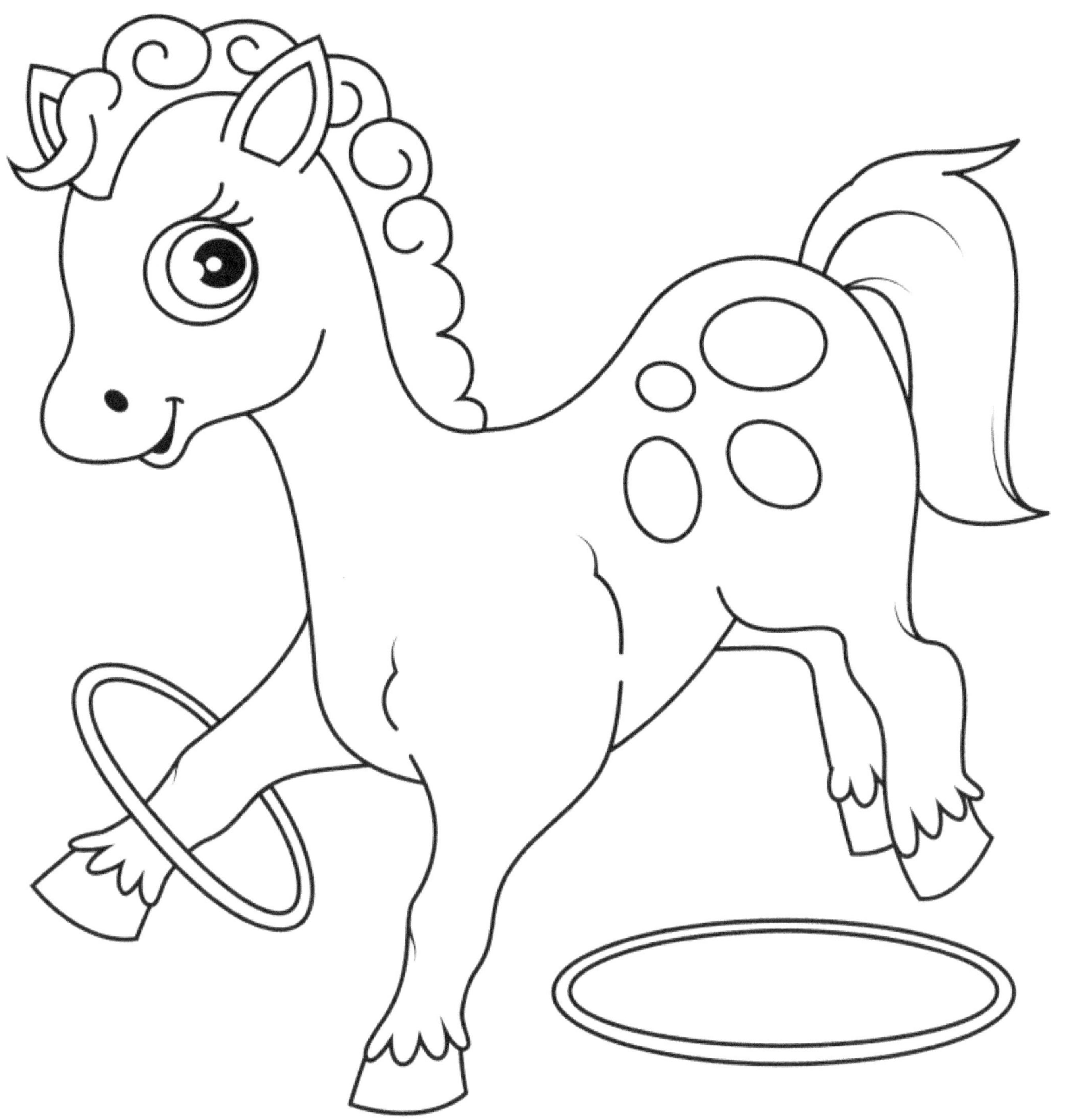

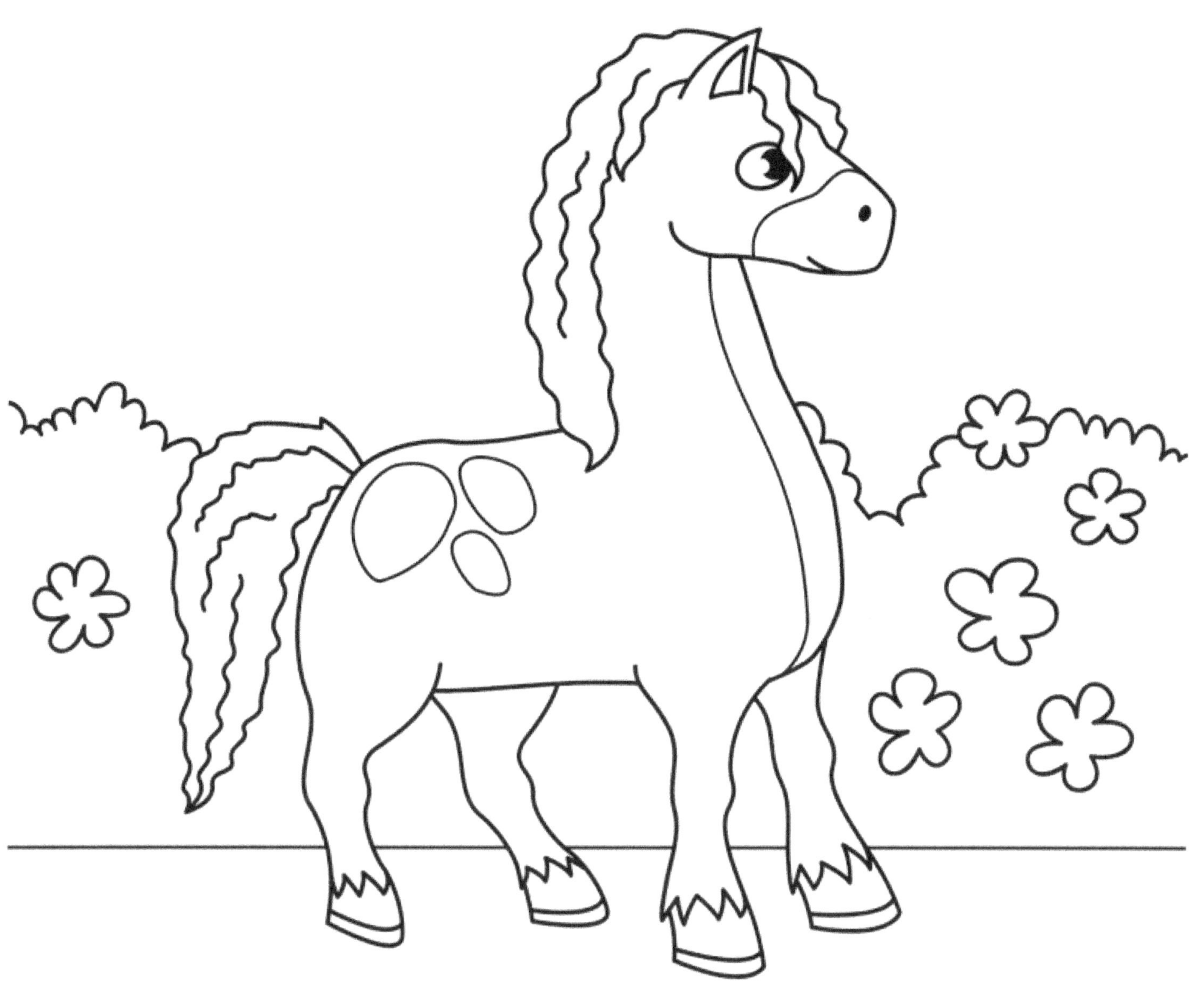

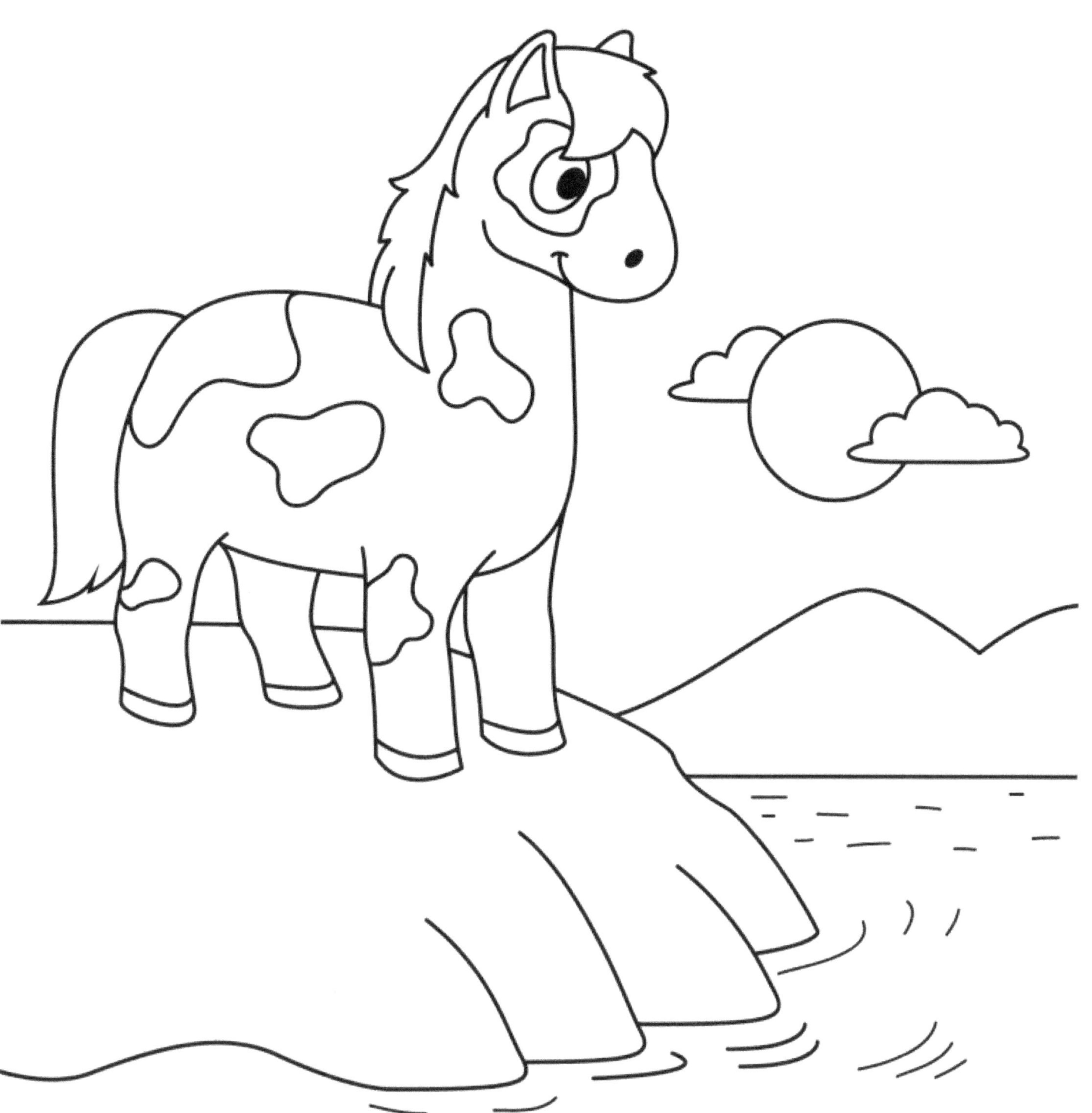

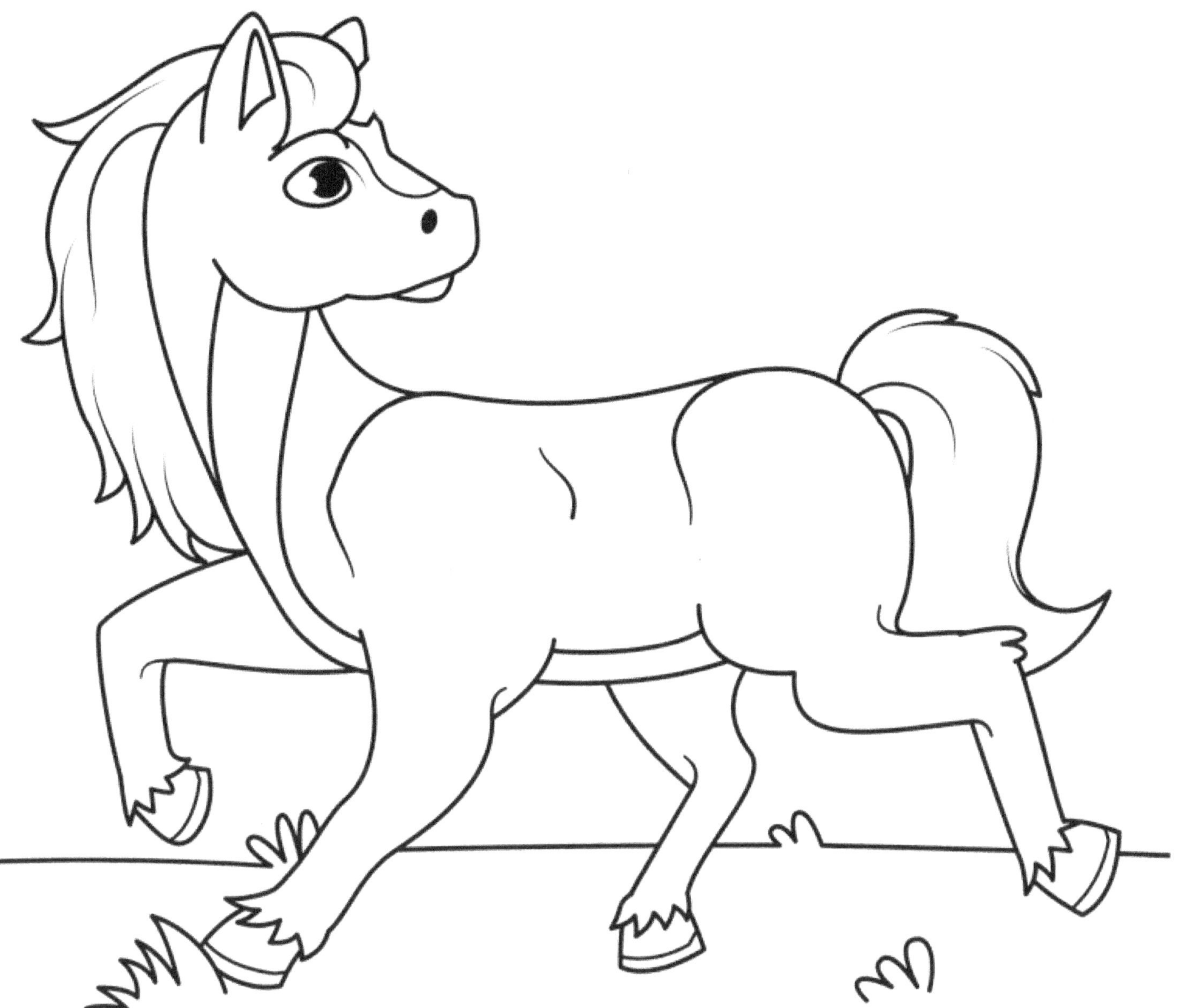

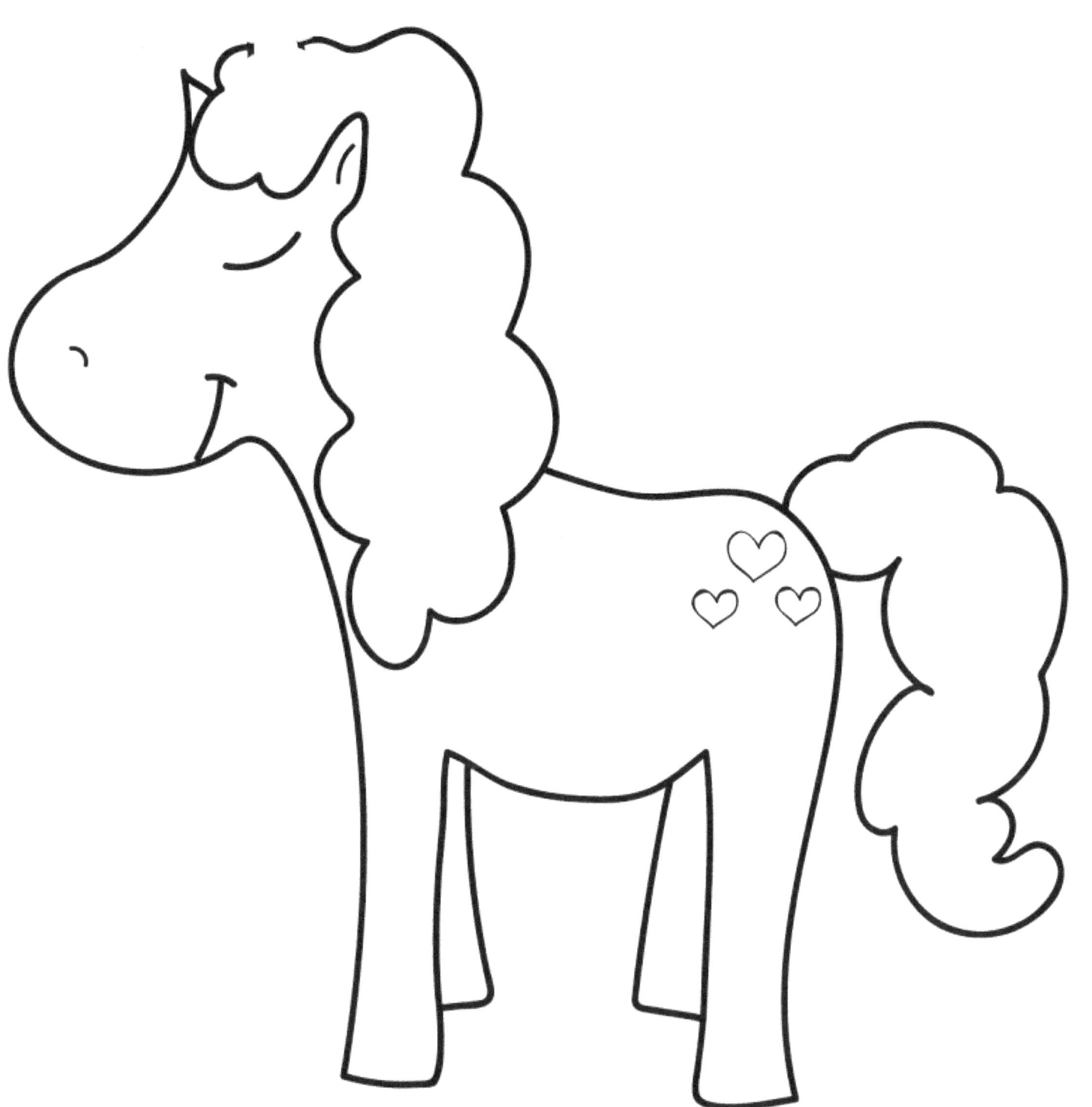

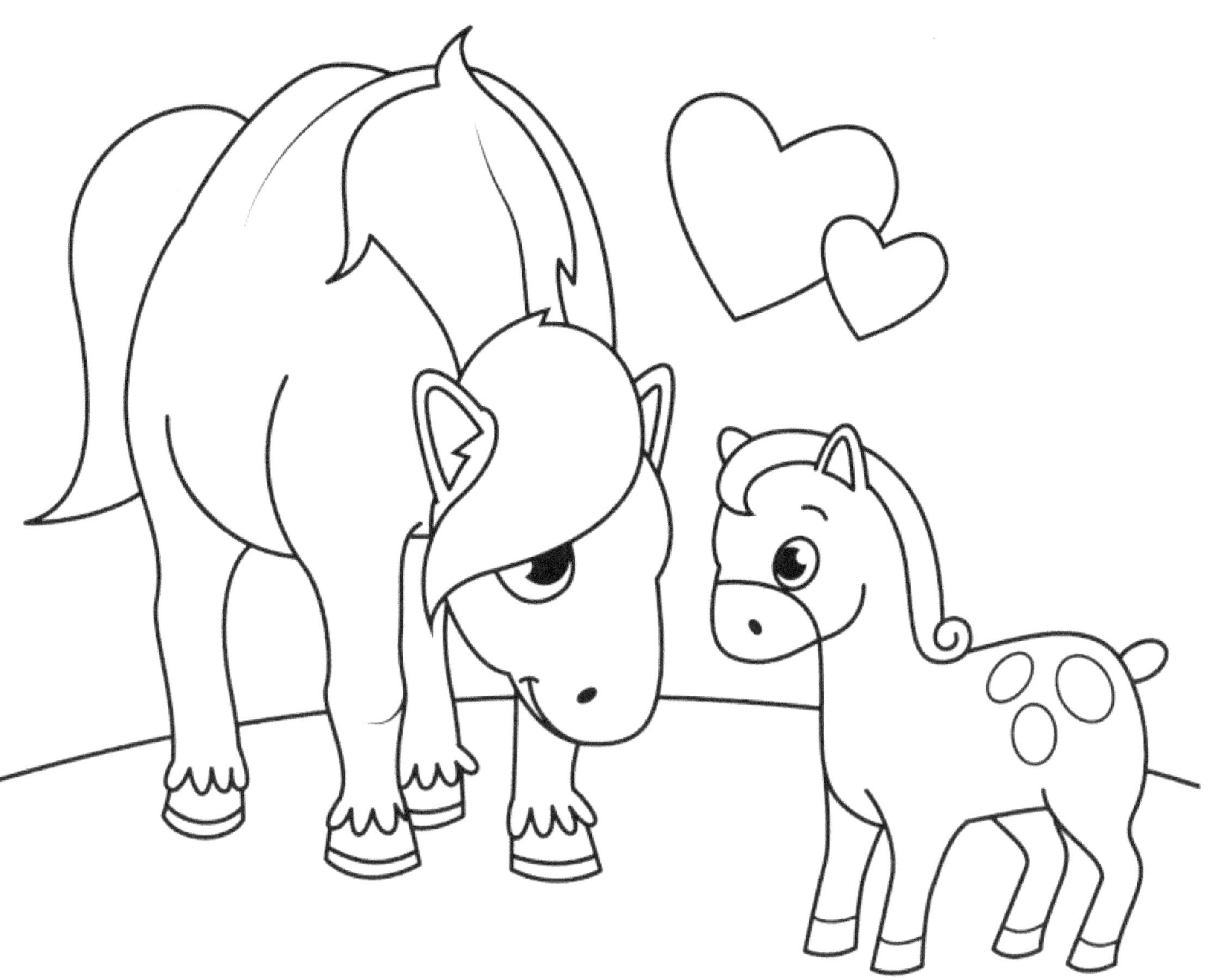

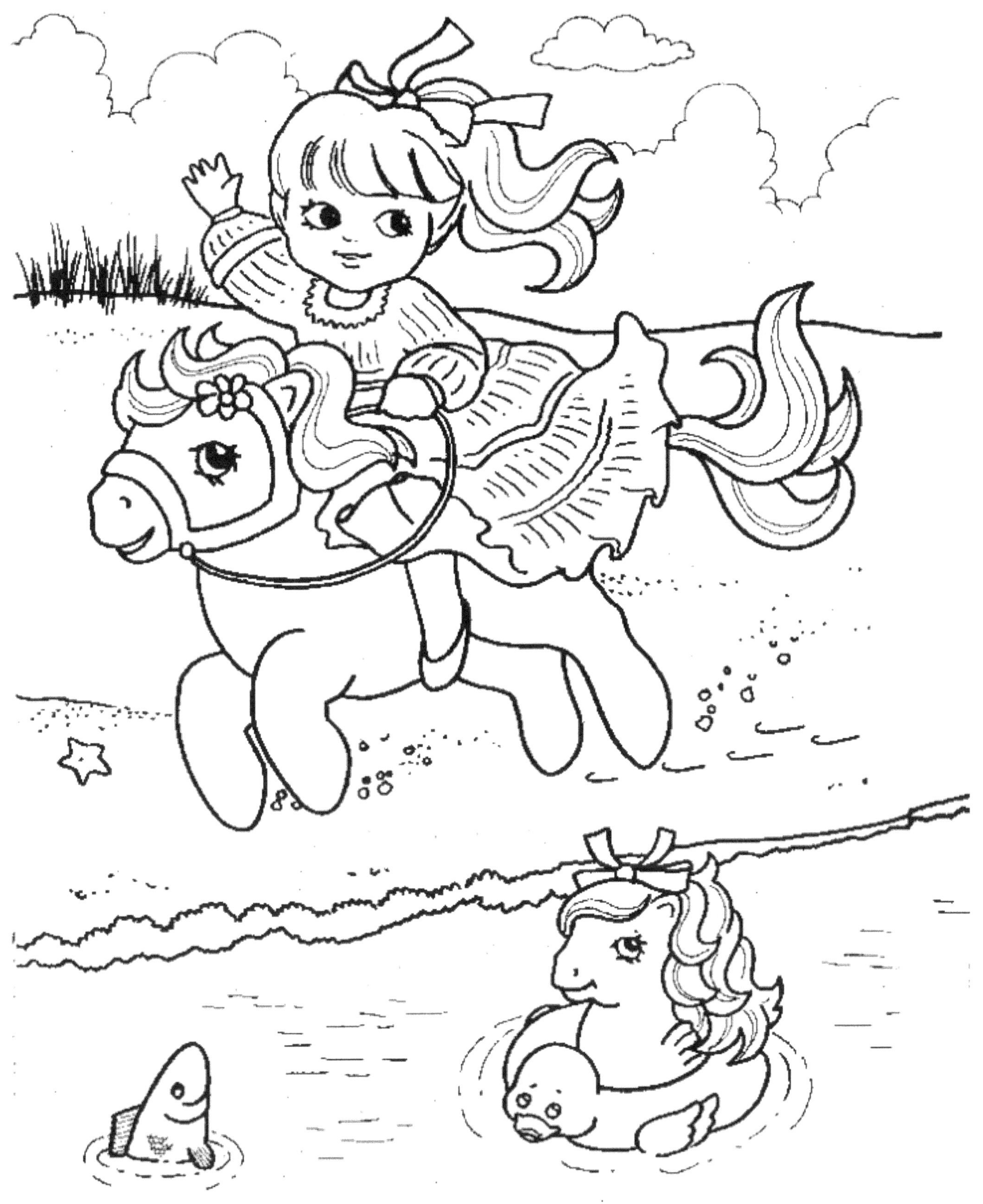

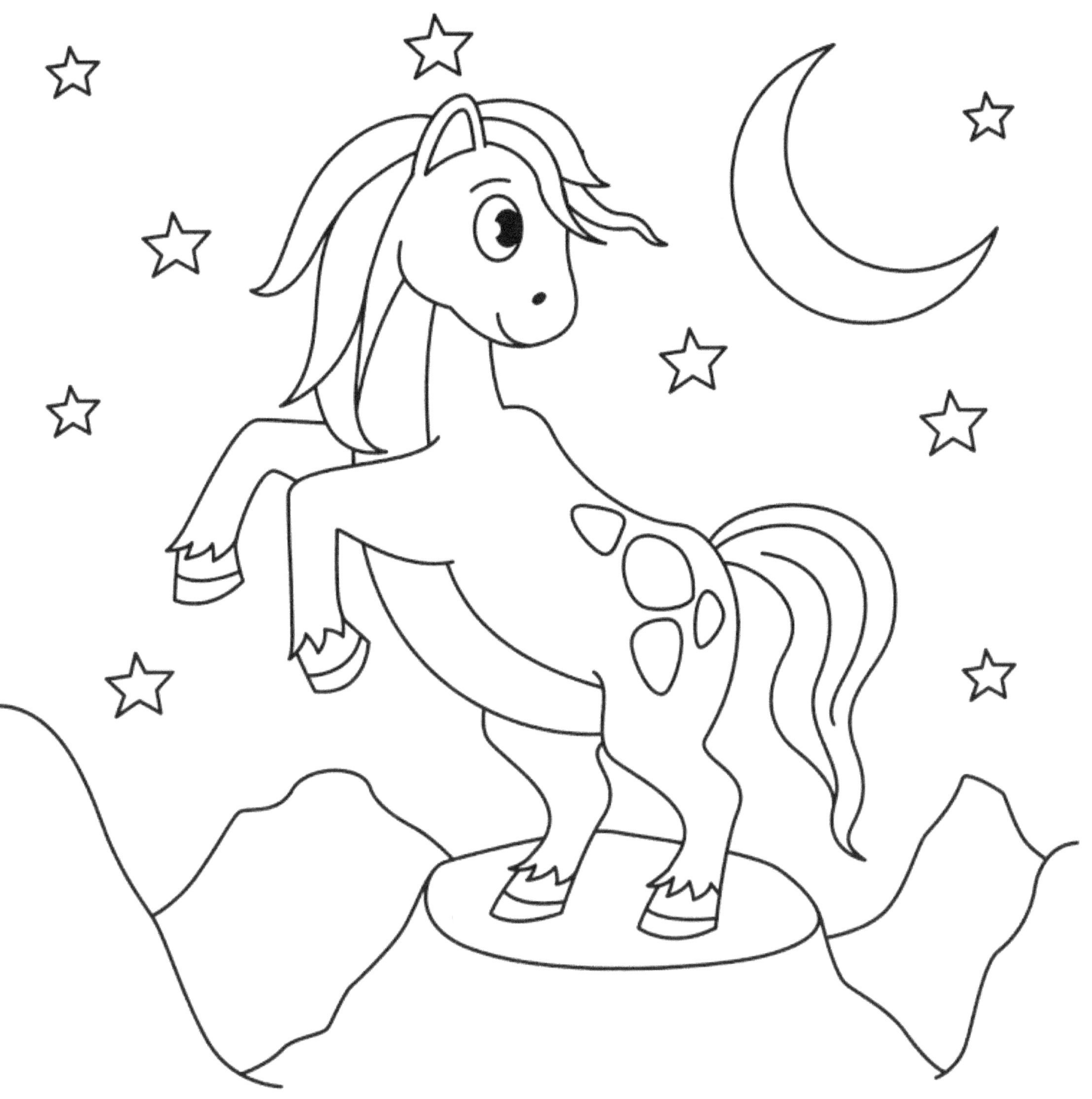

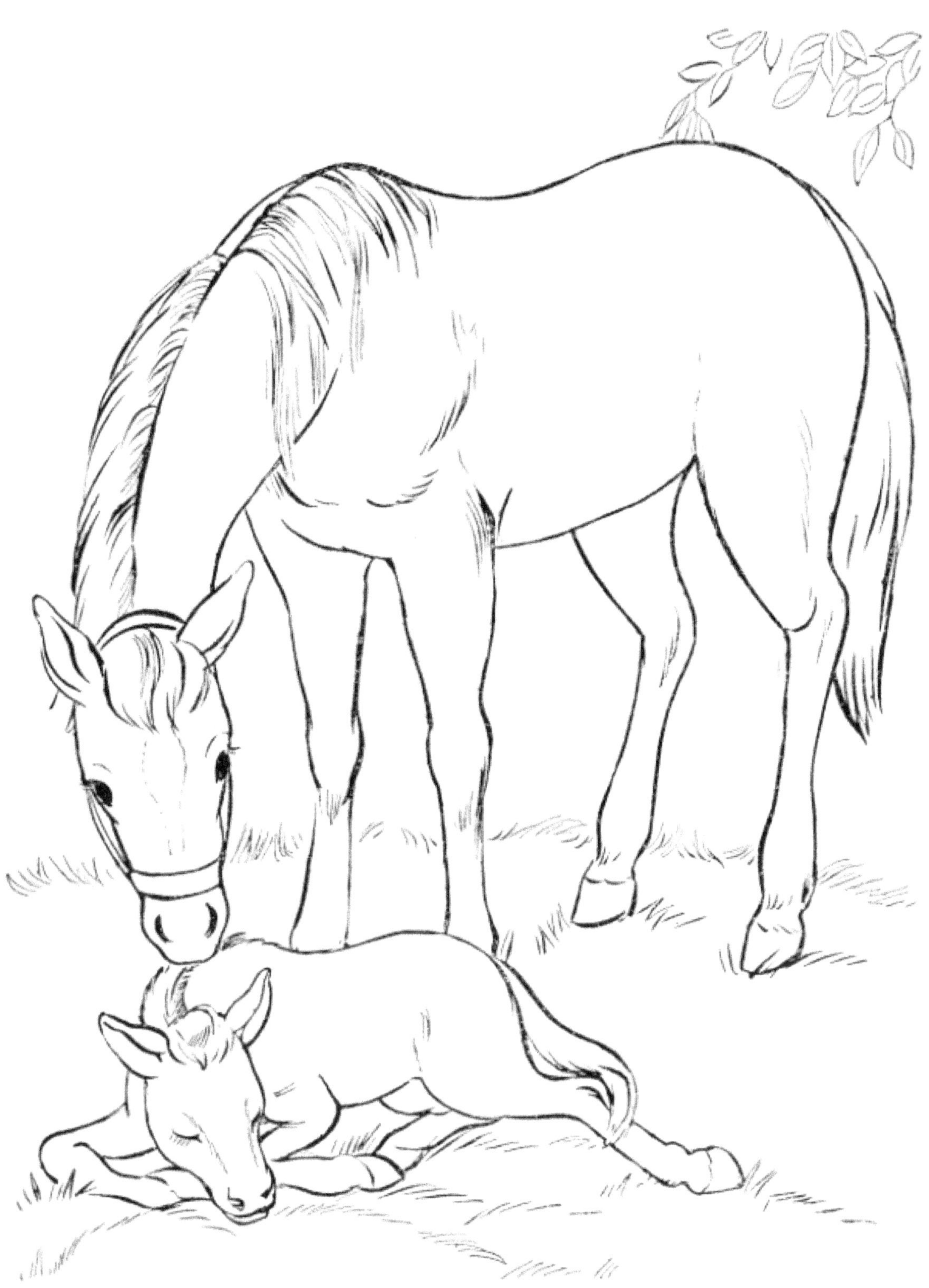

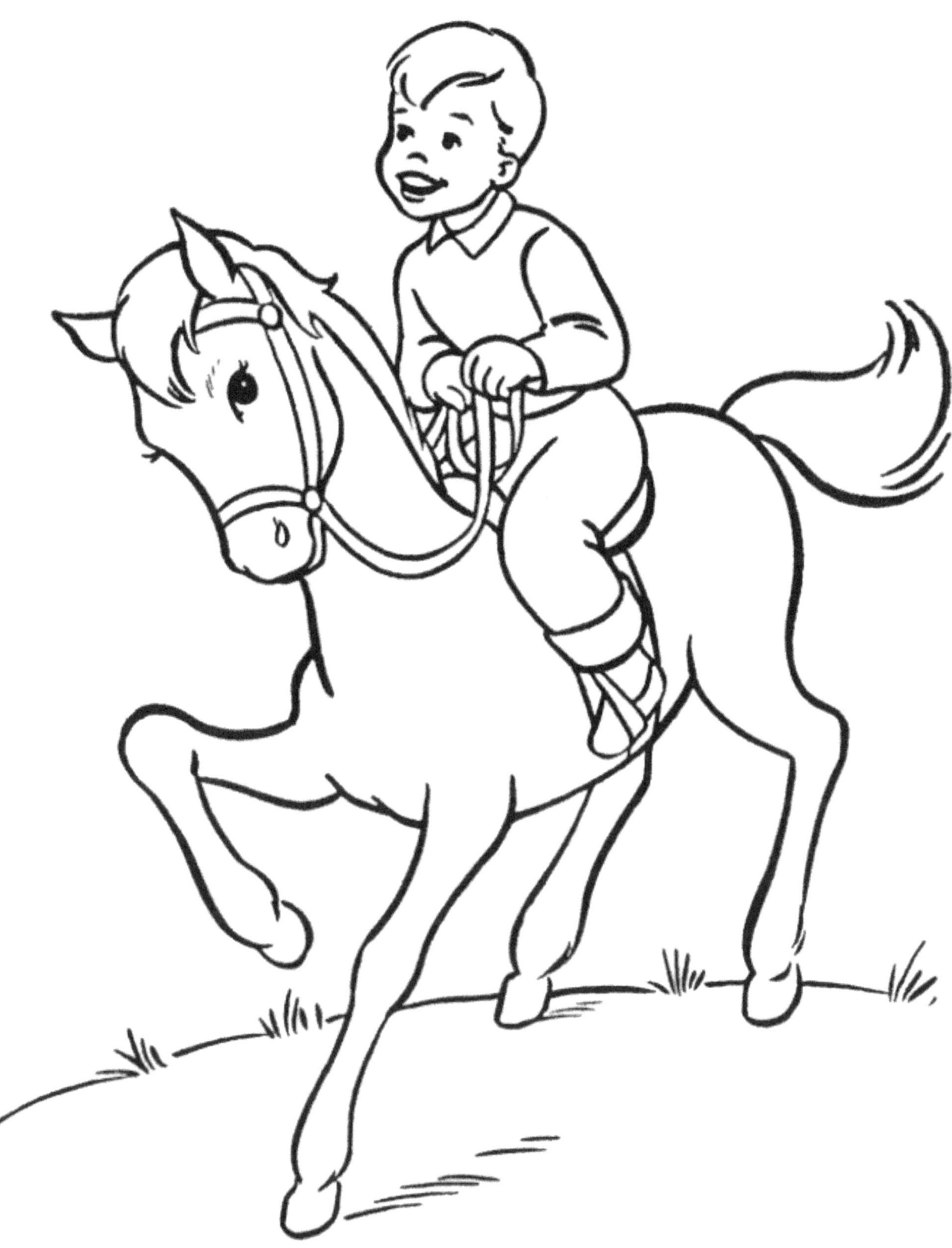

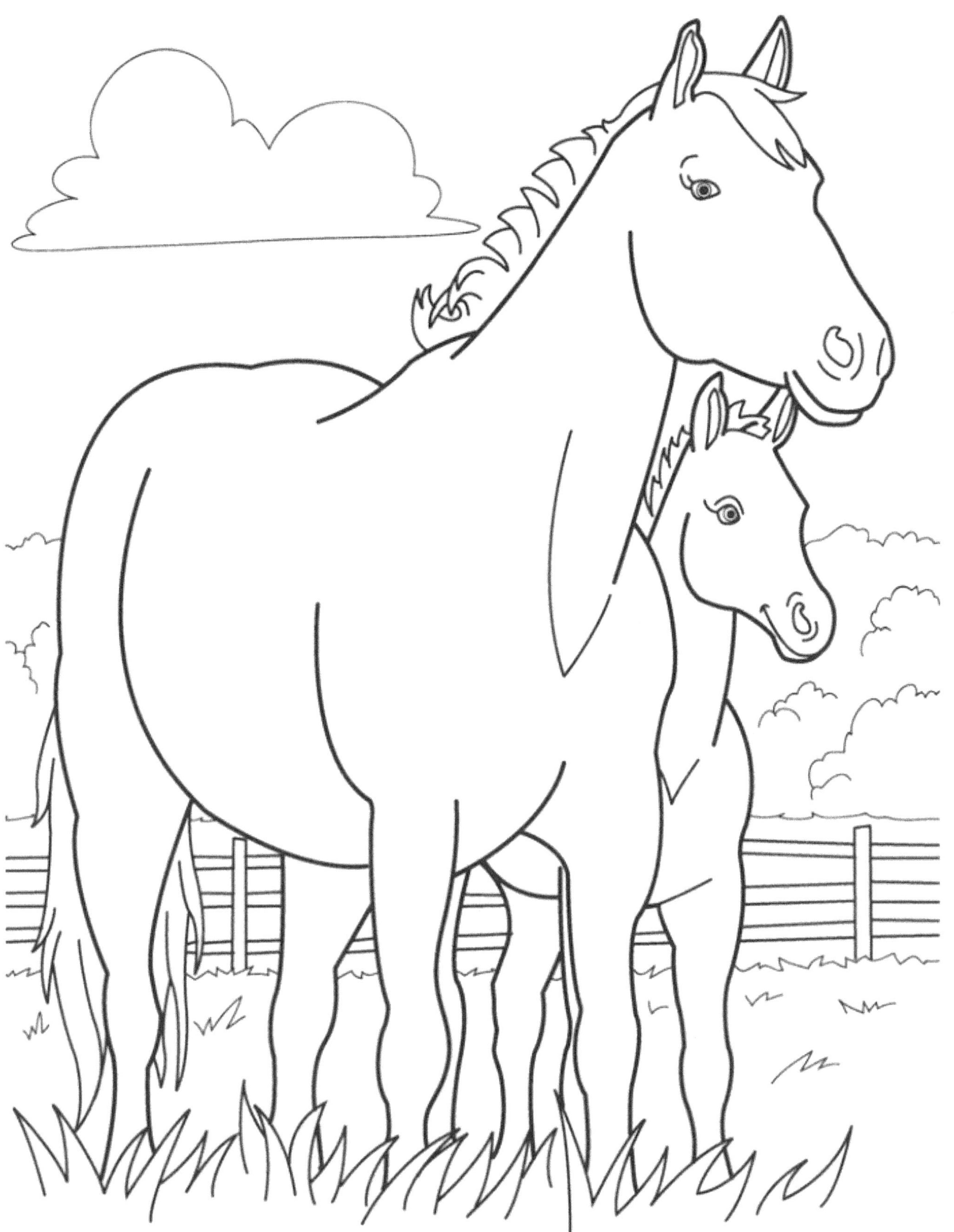

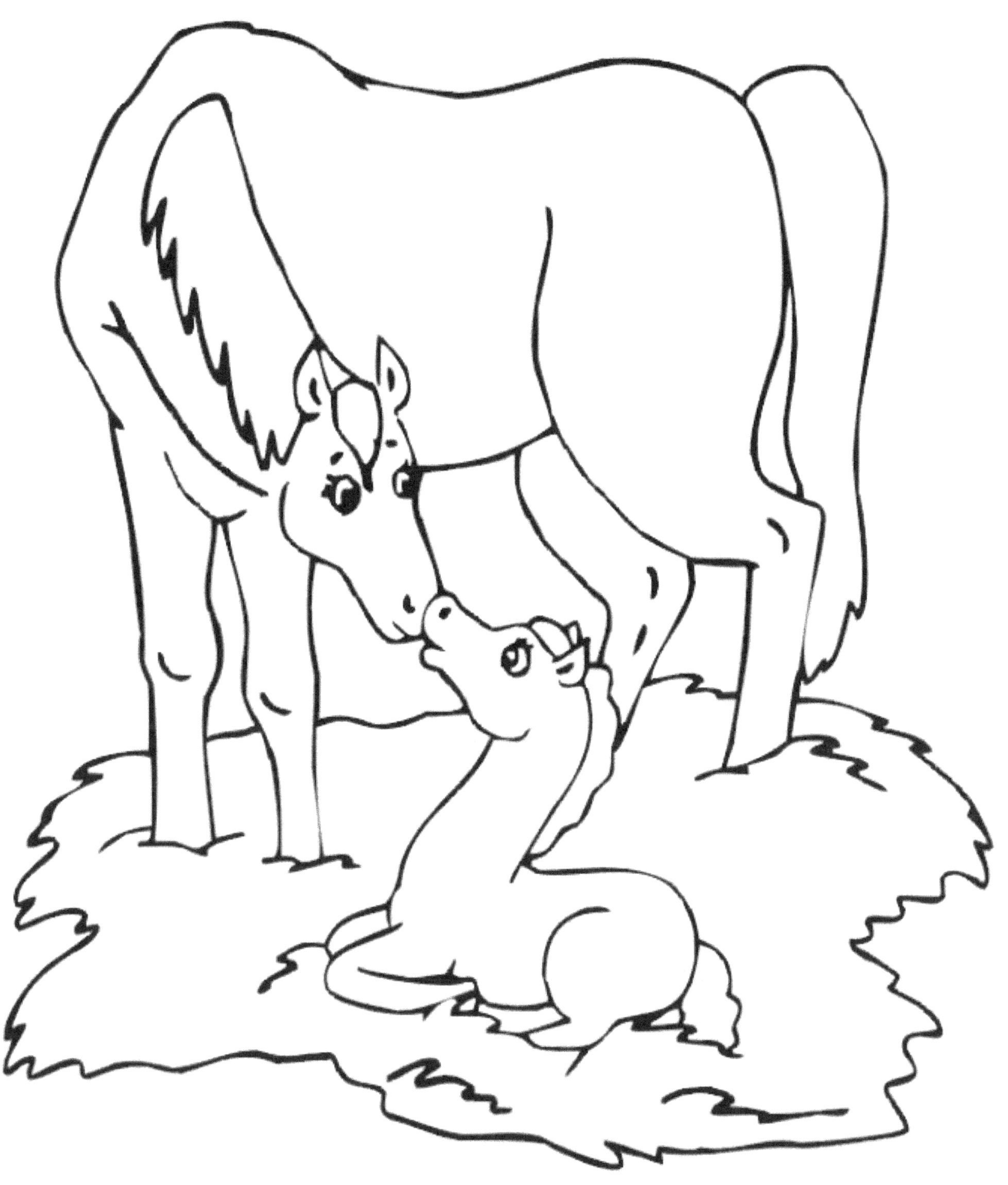

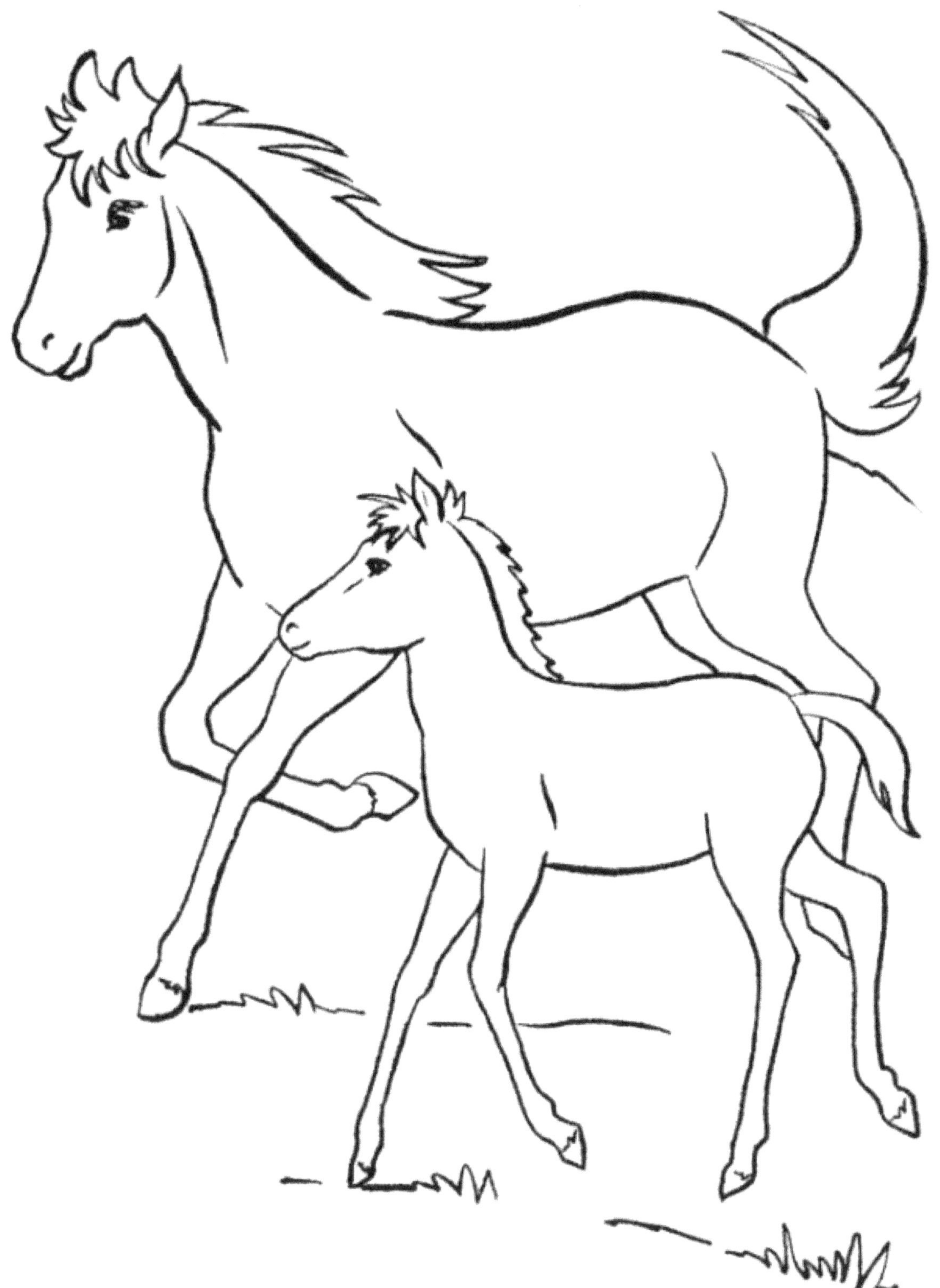

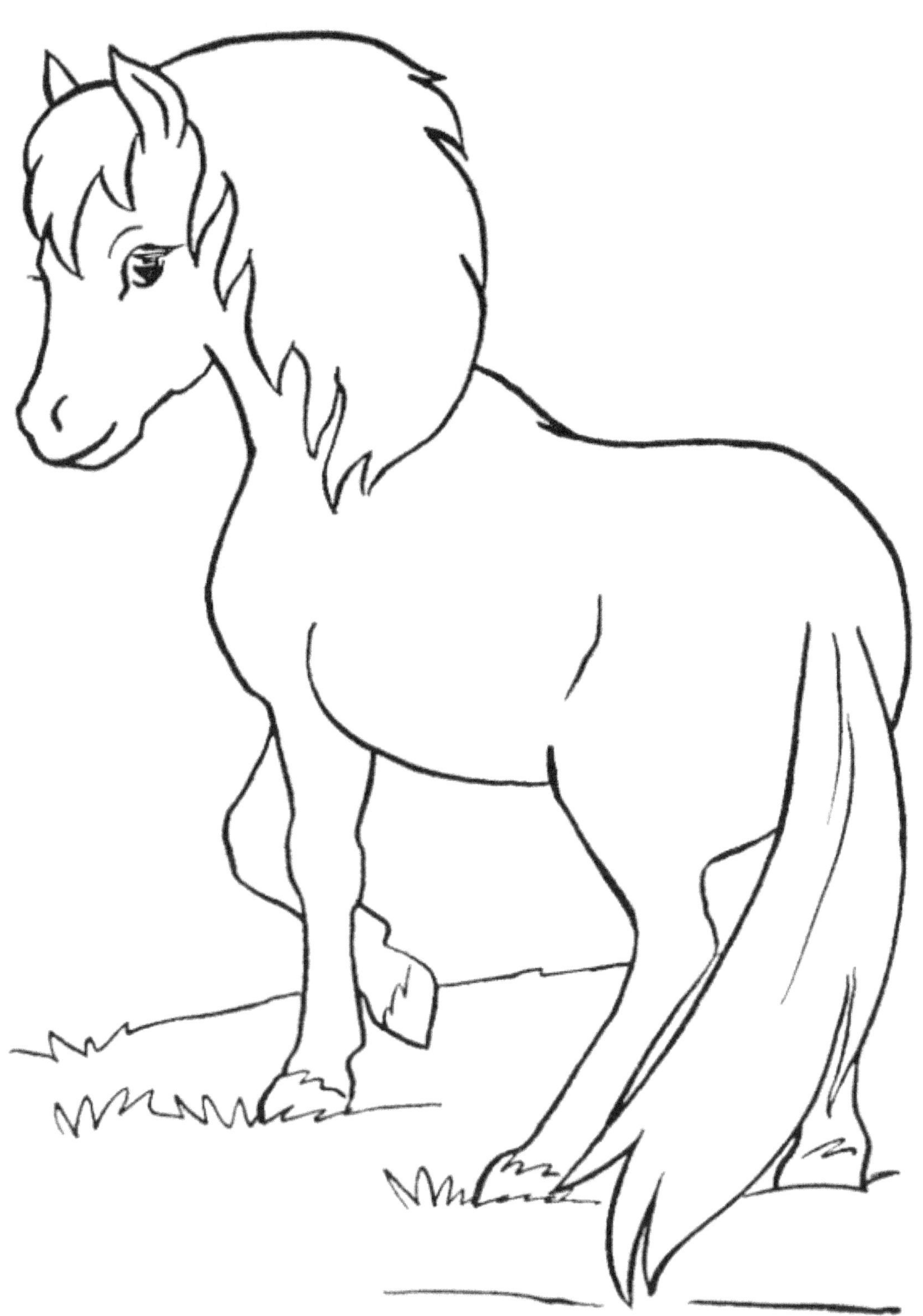

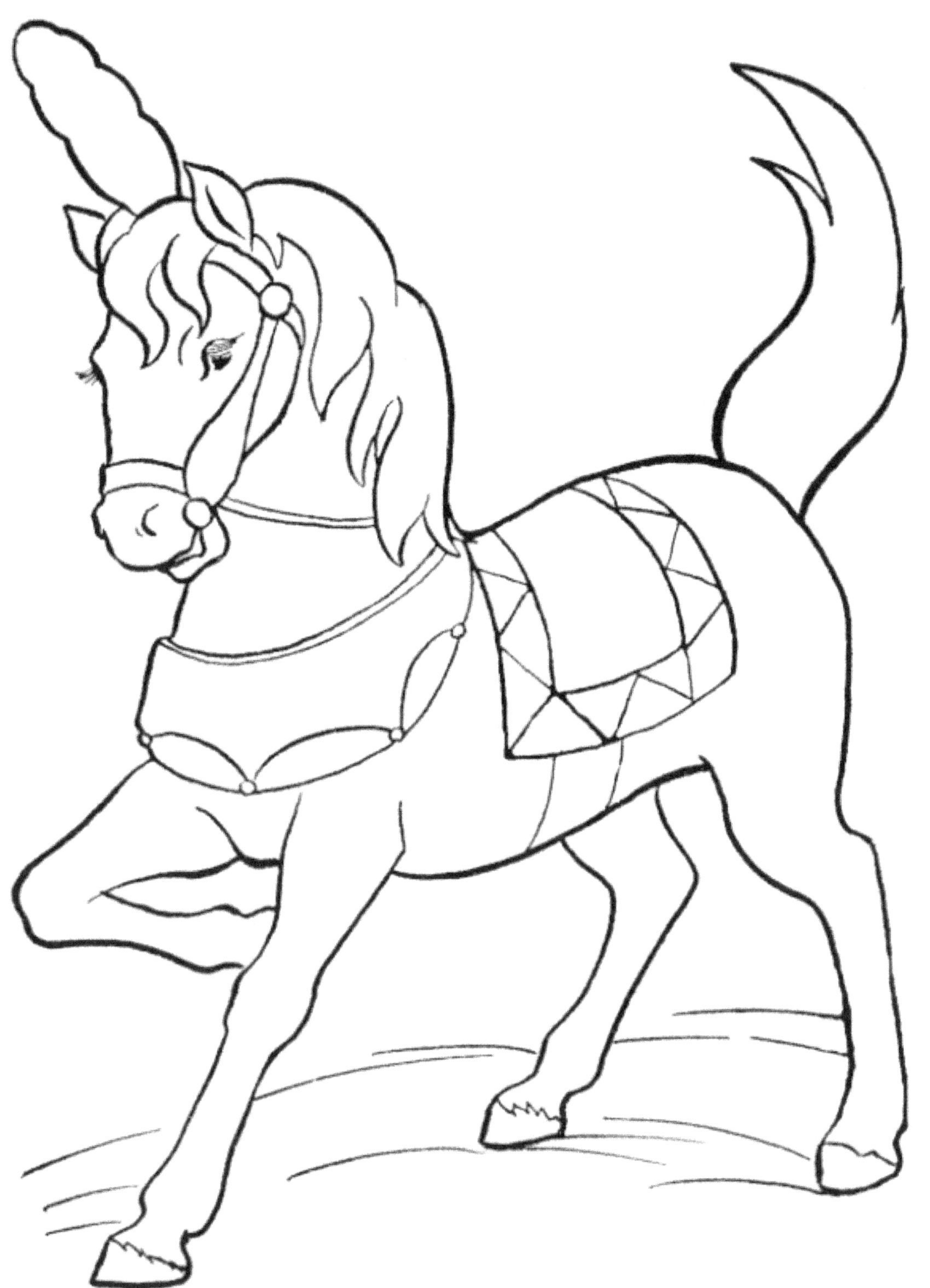

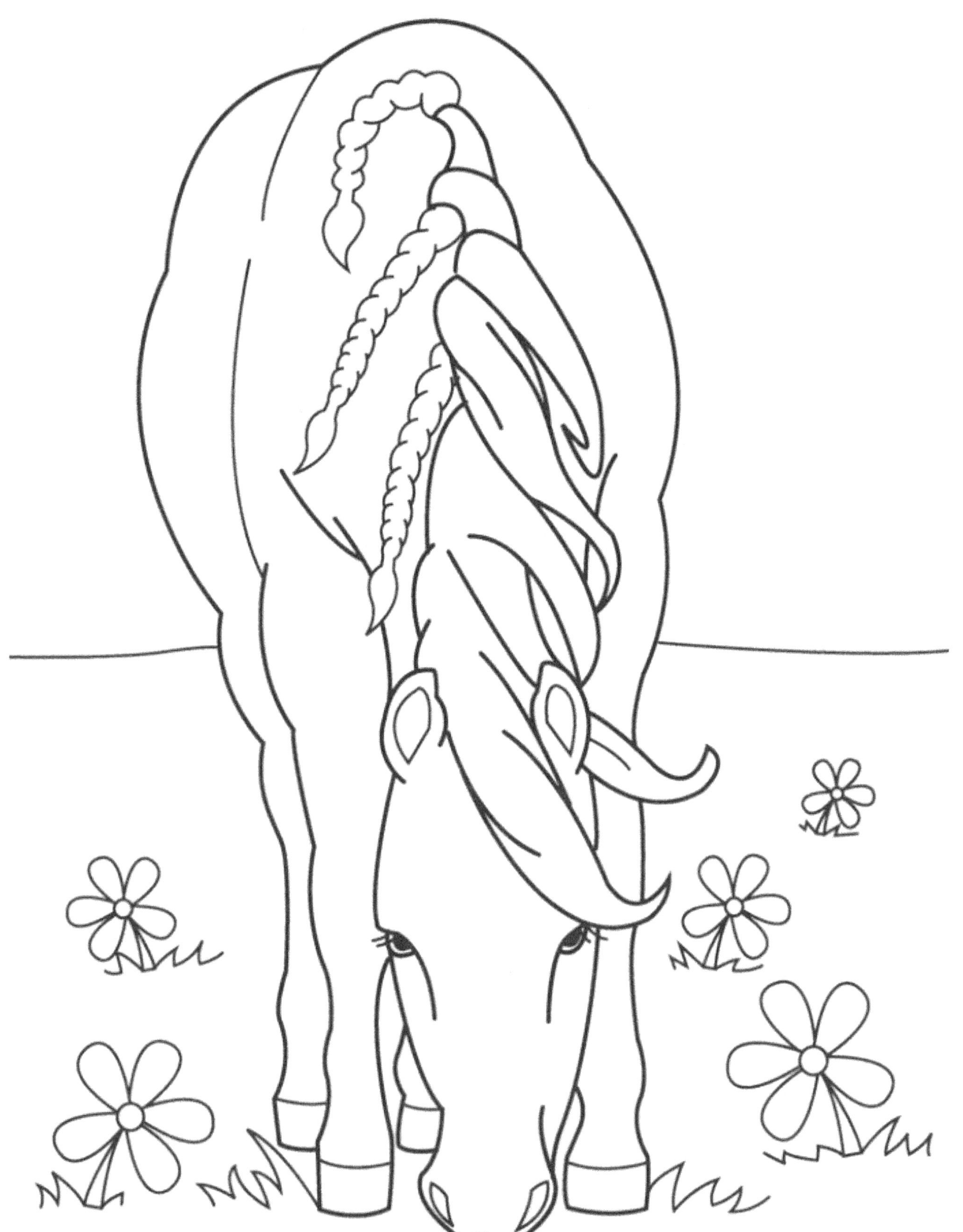

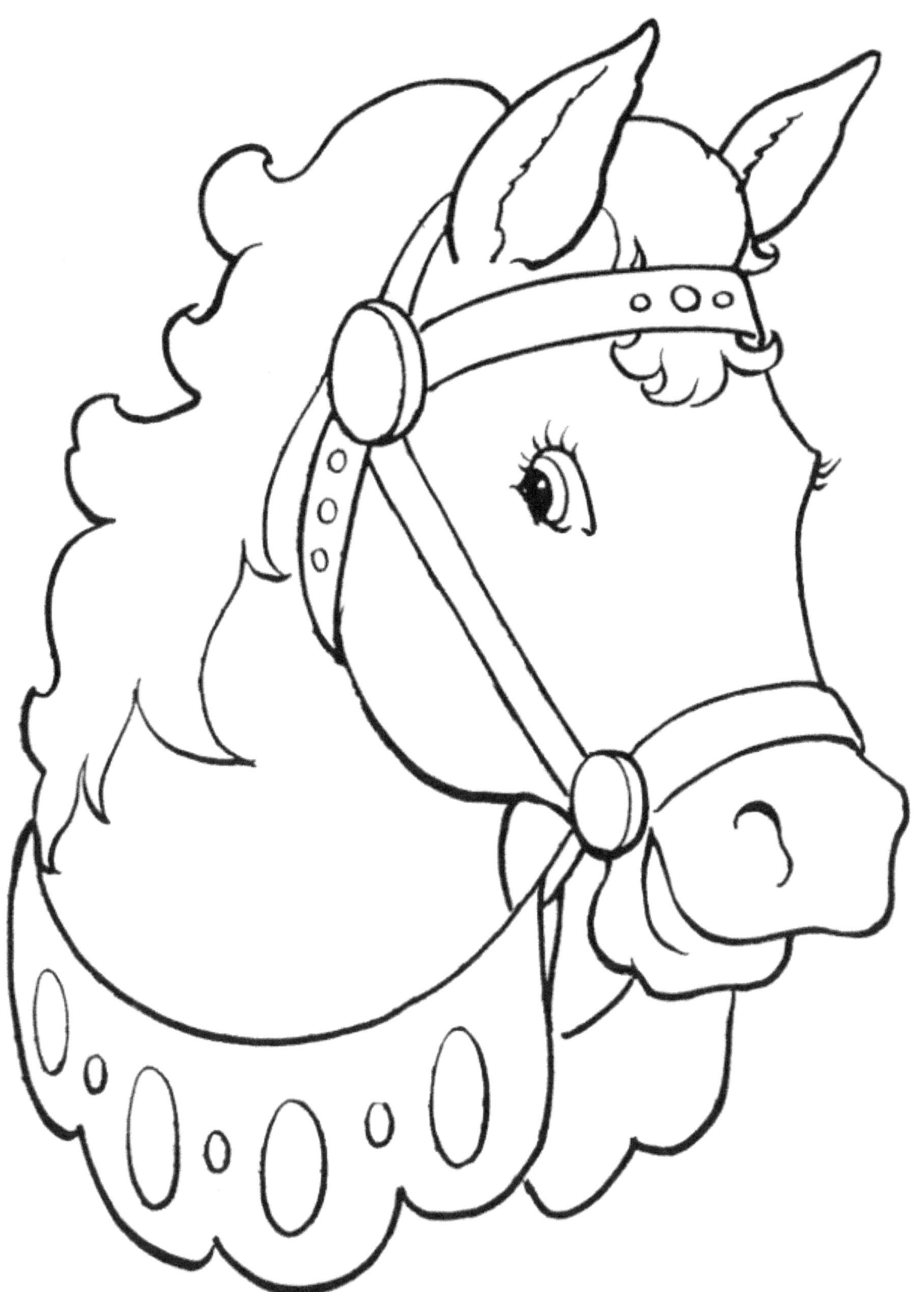

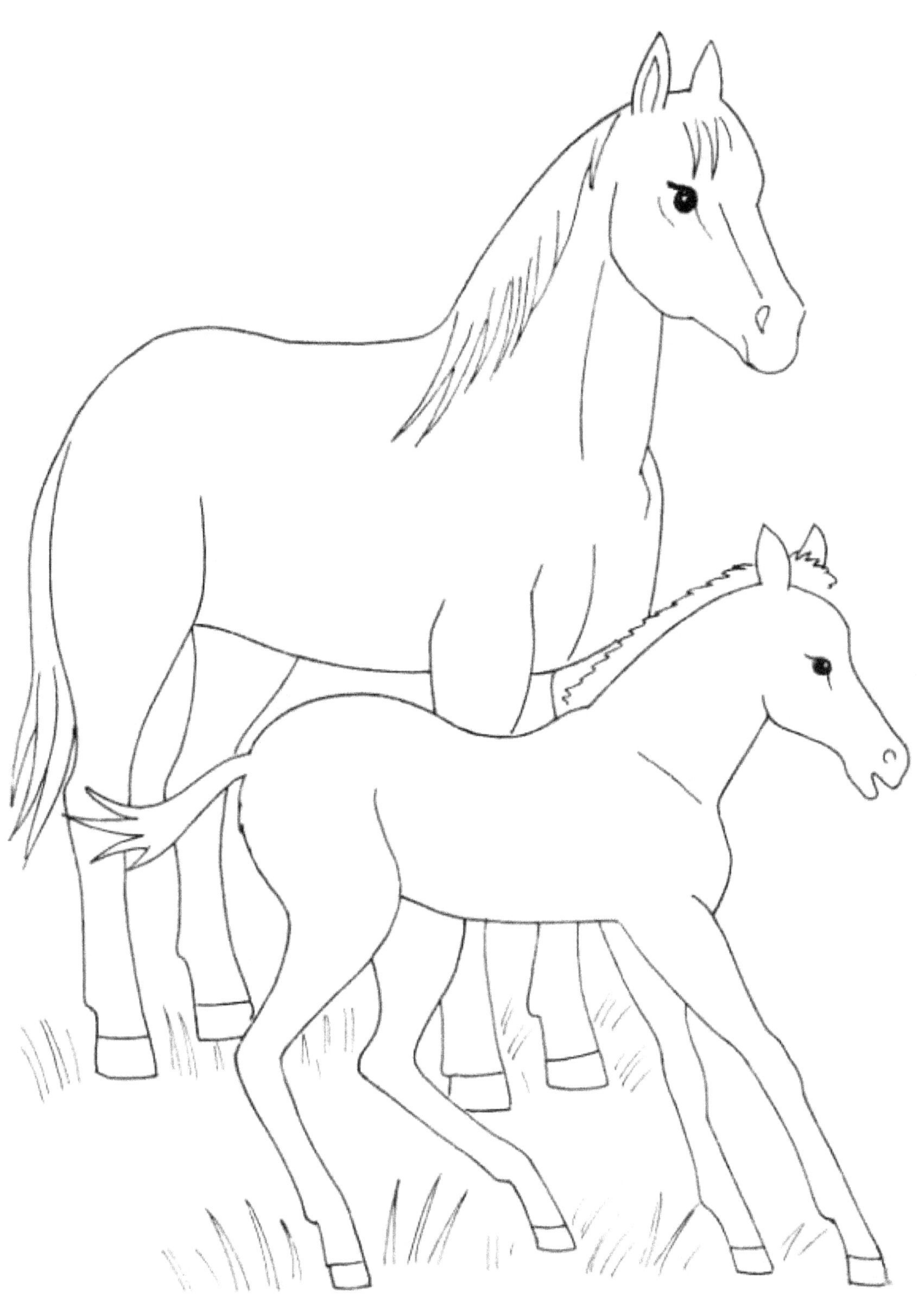

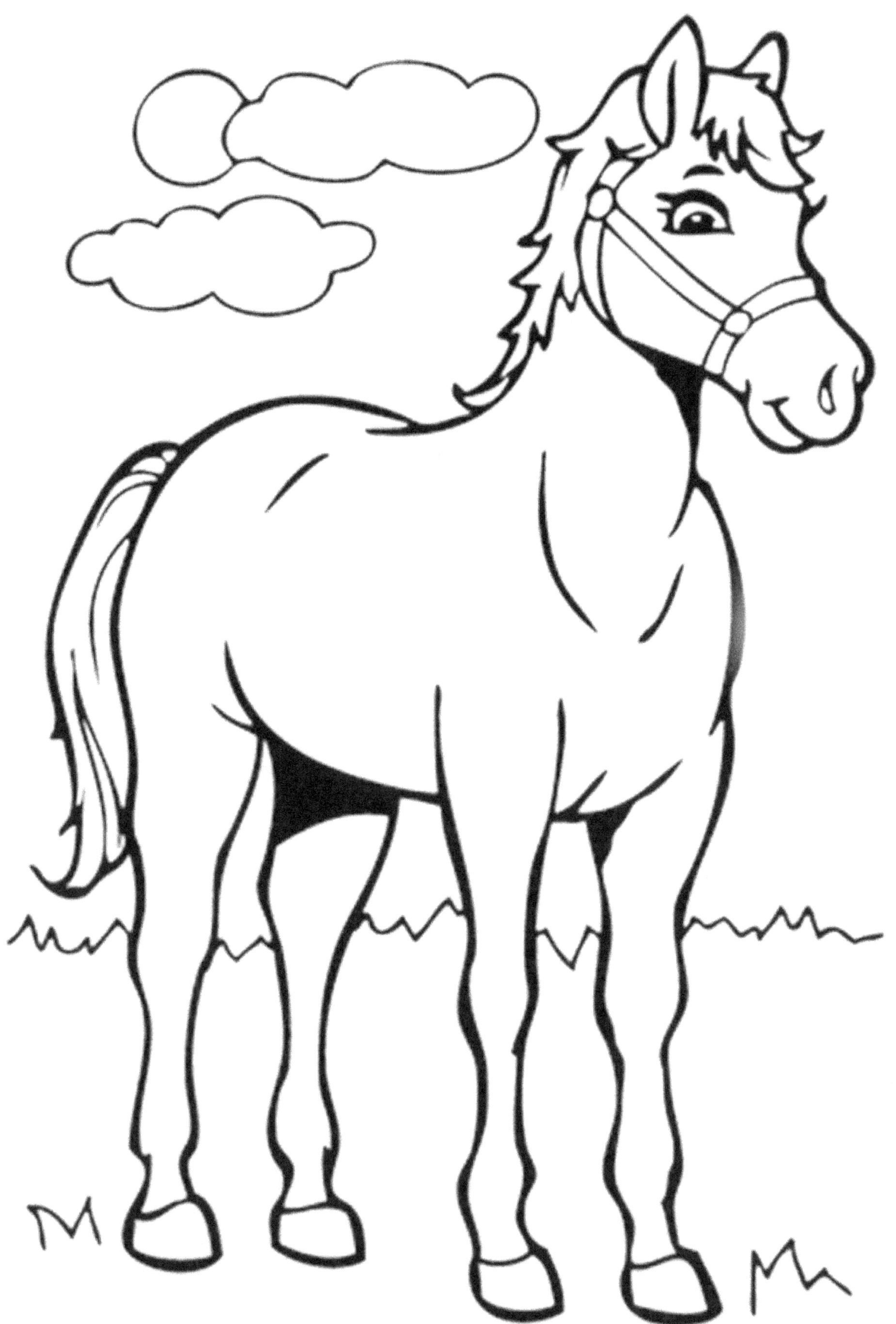

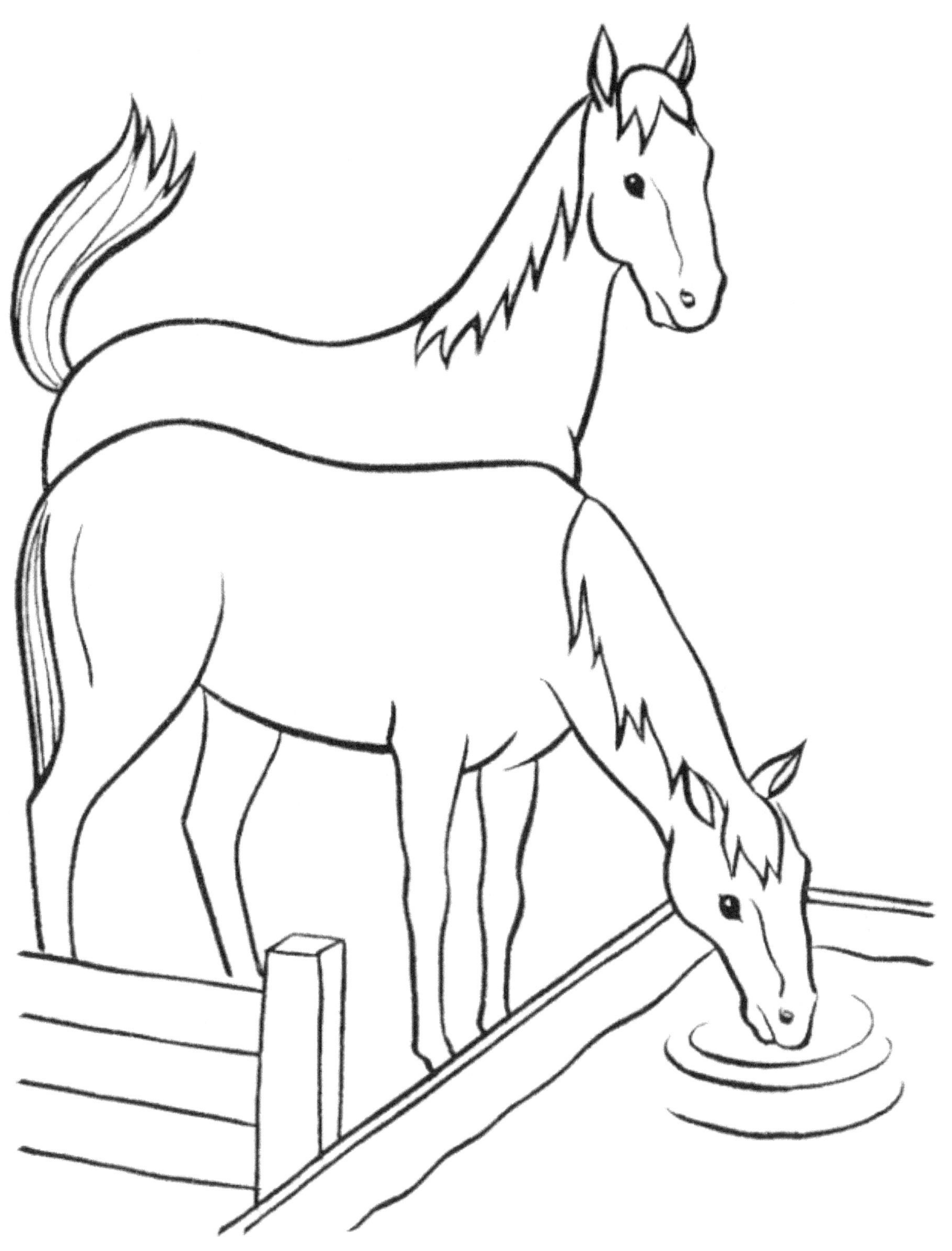

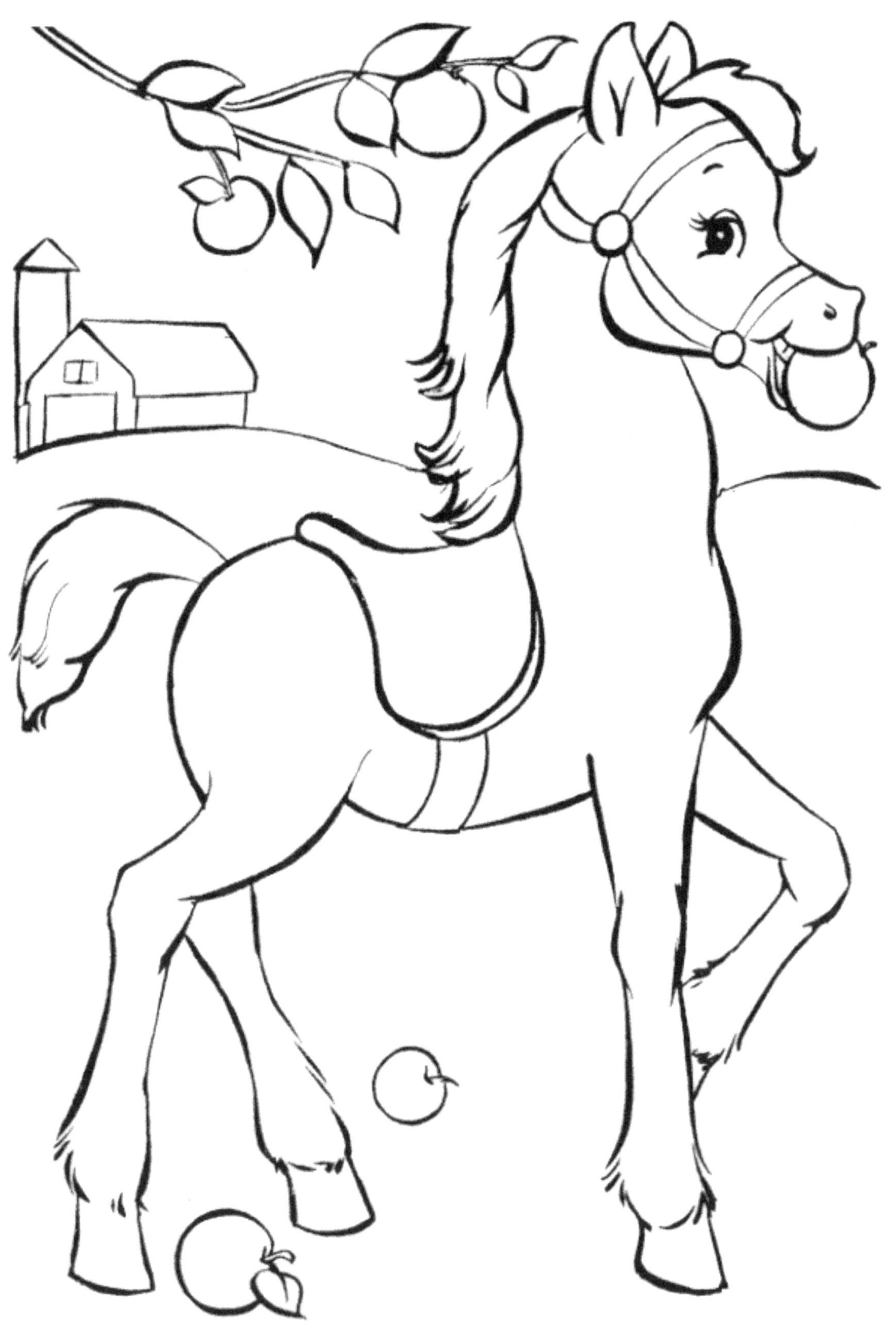

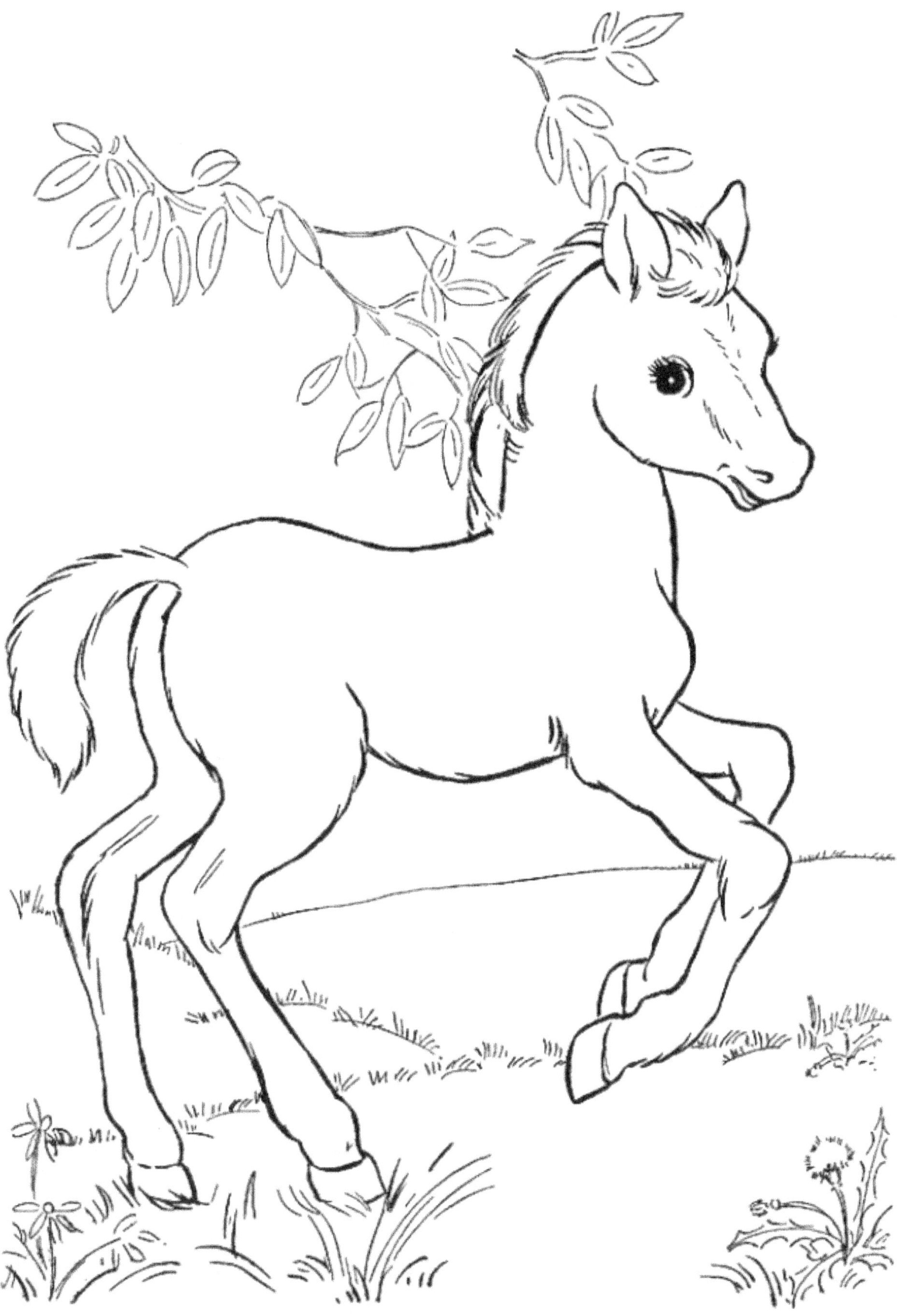

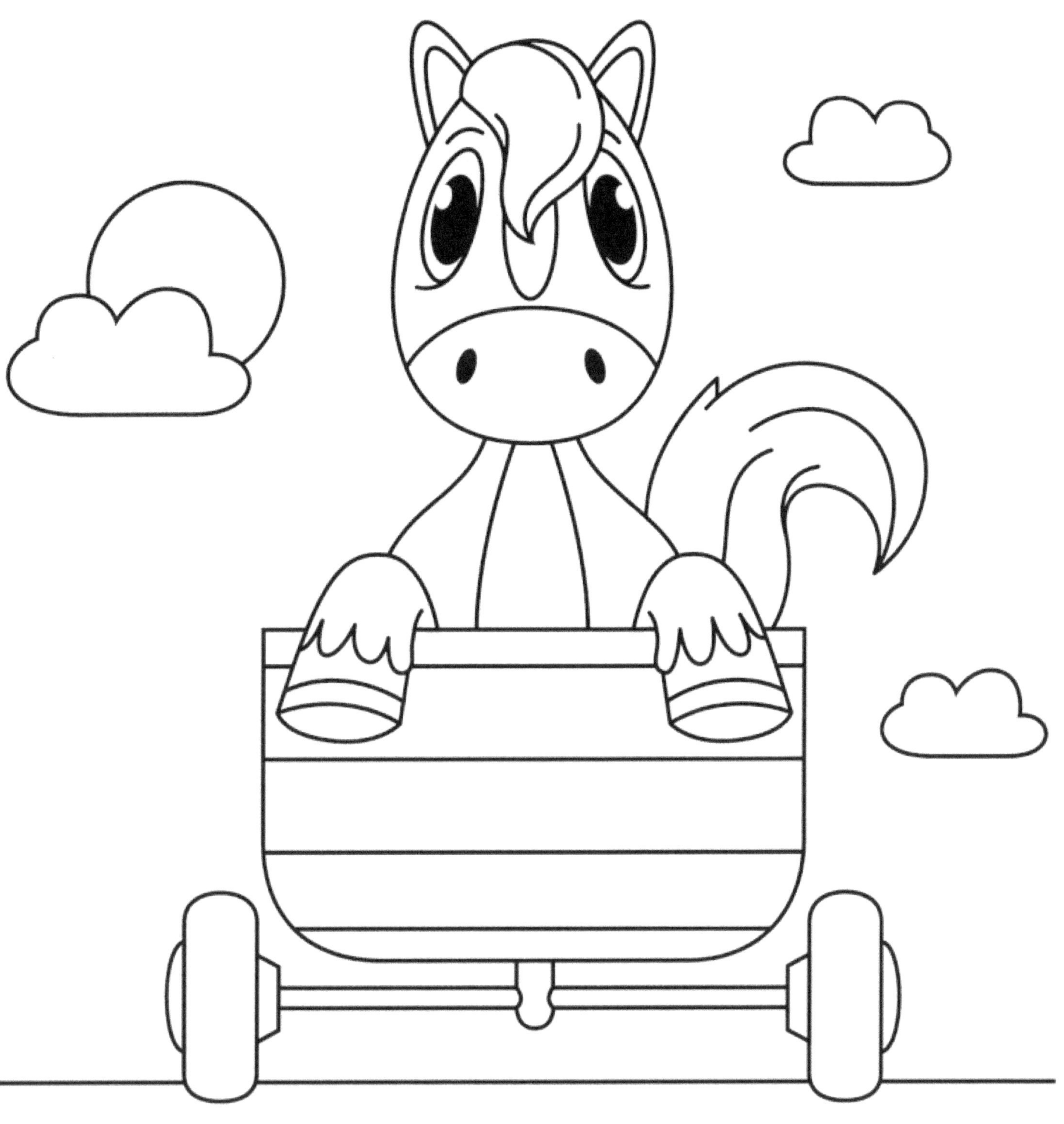

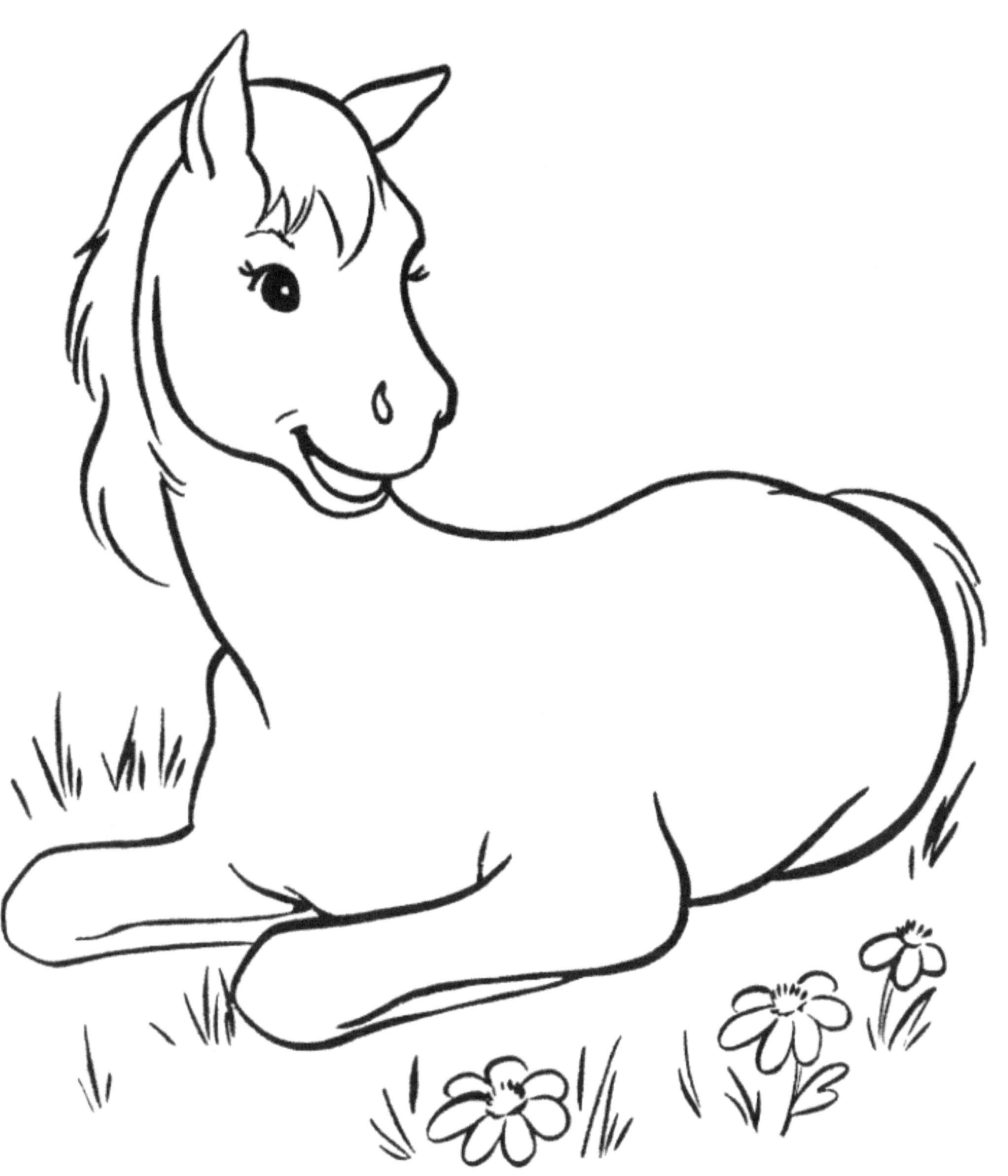